This

DAILY
PLANER

belongs to:

____

____

2021

January

	S	M	T	W	T	F	S
1						**1**	2
2	3	4	5	6	7	8	9
3	10	11	12	13	14	15	16
4	17	**18**	19	20	21	22	23
5	24	25	26	27	28	29	30
6	31						

February

	S	M	T	W	T	F	S
6		1	2	3	4	5	6
7	7	8	9	10	11	12	13
8	14	**15**	16	17	18	19	20
9	21	22	23	24	25	26	27
10	28						

March

	S	M	T	W	T	F	S
10		1	2	3	4	5	6
11	7	8	9	10	11	12	13
12	14	15	16	17	18	19	20
13	21	22	23	24	25	26	27
14	28	29	30	31			

April

	S	M	T	W	T	F	S
14					1	2	3
15	4	5	6	7	8	9	10
16	11	12	13	14	15	16	17
17	18	19	20	21	22	23	24
18	25	26	27	28	29	30	

May

	S	M	T	W	T	F	S
18							1
19	2	3	4	5	6	7	8
20	9	10	11	12	13	14	15
21	16	17	18	19	20	21	22
22	23	24	25	26	27	28	29
23	30	**31**					

June

	S	M	T	W	T	F	S
23			1	2	3	4	5
24	6	7	8	9	10	11	12
25	13	14	15	16	17	18	19
26	20	21	22	23	24	25	26
27	27	28	29	30			

July

	S	M	T	W	T	F	S
27					1	2	3
28	**4**	**5**	6	7	8	9	10
29	11	12	13	14	15	16	17
30	18	19	20	21	22	23	24
31	25	26	27	28	29	30	31

August

	S	M	T	W	T	F	S
32	1	2	3	4	5	6	7
33	8	9	10	11	12	13	14
34	15	16	17	18	19	20	21
35	22	23	24	25	26	27	28
36	29	30	31				

September

	S	M	T	W	T	F	S
36				1	2	3	4
37	5	**6**	7	8	9	10	11
38	12	13	14	15	16	17	18
39	19	20	21	22	23	24	25
40	26	27	28	29	30		

October

	S	M	T	W	T	F	S
40						1	2
41	3	4	5	6	7	8	9
42	10	**11**	12	13	14	15	16
43	17	18	19	20	21	22	23
44	24	25	26	27	28	29	30
45	31						

November

	S	M	T	W	T	F	S
45		1	2	3	4	5	6
46	7	8	9	10	**11**	12	13
47	14	15	16	17	18	19	20
48	21	22	23	24	**25**	26	27
49	28	29	30				

December

	S	M	T	W	T	F	S
49				1	2	3	4
50	5	6	7	8	9	10	11
51	12	13	14	15	16	17	18
52	19	20	21	22	23	**24**	25
1	26	27	28	29	30	**31**	

Jan 1 • New Year's Day
Jan 18 • Martin Luther King Jr. Day
Feb 15 • Presidents' Day (Most regions)
May 31 • Memorial Day
Jul 4 • Independence Day

Jul 5 • 'Independence Day' observed
Sep 6 • Labor Day
Oct 11 • Columbus Day
Nov 11 • Veterans Day
Nov 25 • Thanksgiving Day

Dec 24 • 'Christmas Day' day off
Dec 25 • Christmas Day
Dec 31 • 'New Year's Day' day off

2022

January

	S	M	T	W	T	F	S
1							1
2	2	3	4	5	6	7	8
3	9	10	11	12	13	14	15
4	16	**17**	18	19	20	21	22
5	23	24	25	26	27	28	29
6	30	31					

February

	S	M	T	W	T	F	S
6			1	2	3	4	5
7	6	7	8	9	10	11	12
8	13	14	15	16	17	18	19
9	20	**21**	22	23	24	25	26
10	27	28					

March

	S	M	T	W	T	F	S
10			1	2	3	4	5
11	6	7	8	9	10	11	12
12	13	14	15	16	17	18	19
13	20	21	22	23	24	25	26
14	27	28	29	30	31		

April

	S	M	T	W	T	F	S
14						1	2
15	3	4	5	6	7	8	9
16	10	11	12	13	14	15	16
17	17	18	19	20	21	22	23
18	24	25	26	27	28	29	30

May

	S	M	T	W	T	F	S
19	1	2	3	4	5	6	7
20	8	9	10	11	12	13	14
21	15	16	17	18	19	20	21
22	22	23	24	25	26	27	28
23	29	**30**	31				

June

	S	M	T	W	T	F	S
23				1	2	3	4
24	5	6	7	8	9	10	11
25	12	13	14	15	16	17	18
26	19	20	21	22	23	24	25
27	26	27	28	29	30		

July

	S	M	T	W	T	F	S
27						1	2
28	3	**4**	5	6	7	8	9
29	10	11	12	13	14	15	16
30	17	18	19	20	21	22	23
31	24	25	26	27	28	29	30
32	31						

August

	S	M	T	W	T	F	S
32		1	2	3	4	5	6
33	7	8	9	10	11	12	13
34	14	15	16	17	18	19	20
35	21	22	23	24	25	26	27
36	28	29	30	31			

September

	S	M	T	W	T	F	S
36					1	2	3
37	4	**5**	6	7	8	9	10
38	11	12	13	14	15	16	17
39	18	19	20	21	22	23	24
40	25	26	27	28	29	30	

October

	S	M	T	W	T	F	S
40							1
41	2	3	4	5	6	7	8
42	9	**10**	11	12	13	14	15
43	16	17	18	19	20	21	22
44	23	24	25	26	27	28	29
45	30	31					

November

	S	M	T	W	T	F	S
45			1	2	3	4	5
46	6	7	8	9	10	**11**	12
47	13	14	15	16	17	18	19
48	20	21	22	23	**24**	25	26
49	27	28	29	30			

December

	S	M	T	W	T	F	S
49					1	2	3
50	4	5	6	7	8	9	10
51	11	12	13	14	15	16	17
52	18	19	20	21	22	23	24
53	25	**26**	27	28	29	30	31

Jan 1 • New Year's Day
Jan 17 • Martin Luther King Jr. Day
Feb 21 • Presidents' Day (Most regions)
May 30 • Memorial Day

Jul 4 • Independence Day
Sep 5 • Labor Day
Oct 10 • Columbus Day
Nov 11 • Veterans Day

Nov 24 • Thanksgiving Day
Dec 25 • Christmas Day
Dec 26 • 'Christmas Day' day off

Friday

January 1st, 2021

5	
6	
7	
8	
9	
10	
11	
12pm	
1	
2	
3	
4	
5	
6	
7	
8	

PRIORITIES

TO DO

NOTES:

Saturday

January 2nd, 2021

5	
6	
7	
8	
9	
10	
11	
12pm	
1	
2	
3	
4	
5	
6	
7	
8	

PRIORITIES

TO DO

NOTES:

Sunday

January 3rd, 2021

5	
6	
7	
8	
9	
10	
11	
12pm	
1	
2	
3	
4	
5	
6	
7	
8	

PRIORITIES

TO DO

NOTES:

Monday

January 4th, 2021

5	
6	
7	
8	
9	
10	
11	
12pm	
1	
2	
3	
4	
5	
6	
7	
8	

PRIORITIES

TO DO

NOTES:

Tuesday

January 5th, 2021

5	
6	
7	
8	
9	
10	
11	
12pm	
1	
2	
3	
4	
5	
6	
7	
8	

PRIORITIES

TO DO

NOTES:

Wednesday

January 6th, 2021

5	
6	
7	
8	
9	
10	
11	
12pm	
1	
2	
3	
4	
5	
6	
7	
8	

PRIORITIES

TO DO

NOTES:

Thursday

January 7th, 2021

5	
6	
7	
8	
9	
10	
11	
12pm	
1	
2	
3	
4	
5	
6	
7	
8	

PRIORITIES

TO DO

NOTES:

Friday

January 8th, 2021

5	
6	
7	
8	
9	
10	
11	
12pm	
1	
2	
3	
4	
5	
6	
7	
8	

PRIORITIES

TO DO

NOTES:

Saturday

January 9th, 2021

5	
6	
7	
8	
9	
10	
11	
12pm	
1	
2	
3	
4	
5	
6	
7	
8	

PRIORITIES

TO DO

NOTES:

Sunday

January 10th, 2021

5	
6	
7	
8	
9	
10	
11	
12pm	
1	
2	
3	
4	
5	
6	
7	
8	

PRIORITIES

TO DO

NOTES:

Monday

January 11th, 2021

5	
6	
7	
8	
9	
10	
11	
12pm	
1	
2	
3	
4	
5	
6	
7	
8	

PRIORITIES

TO DO

NOTES:

Tuesday

January 12th, 2021

5	
6	
7	
8	
9	
10	
11	
12pm	
1	
2	
3	
4	
5	
6	
7	
8	

PRIORITIES

TO DO

NOTES:

Wednesday

January 13th, 2021

5	
6	
7	
8	
9	
10	
11	
12pm	
1	
2	
3	
4	
5	
6	
7	
8	

PRIORITIES

TO DO

NOTES:

Thursday

January 14th, 2021

5	
6	
7	
8	
9	
10	
11	
12pm	
1	
2	
3	
4	
5	
6	
7	
8	

PRIORITIES

TO DO

NOTES:

Friday

January 15th, 2021

5	
6	
7	
8	
9	
10	
11	
12pm	
1	
2	
3	
4	
5	
6	
7	
8	

PRIORITIES

TO DO

NOTES:

Saturday

January 16th, 2021

5	
6	
7	
8	
9	
10	
11	
12pm	
1	
2	
3	
4	
5	
6	
7	
8	

PRIORITIES

TO DO

NOTES:

Sunday

January 17th, 2021

5	
6	
7	
8	
9	
10	
11	
12pm	
1	
2	
3	
4	
5	
6	
7	
8	

PRIORITIES

TO DO

NOTES:

Monday

January 18th, 2021

5	
6	
7	
8	
9	
10	
11	
12pm	
1	
2	
3	
4	
5	
6	
7	
8	

PRIORITIES

TO DO

NOTES:

Tuesday

January 19th, 2021

5	
6	
7	
8	
9	
10	
11	
12pm	
1	
2	
3	
4	
5	
6	
7	
8	

PRIORITIES

TO DO

NOTES:

Wednesday

January 20th, 2021

5	
6	
7	
8	
9	
10	
11	
12pm	
1	
2	
3	
4	
5	
6	
7	
8	

PRIORITIES

TO DO

NOTES:

Thursday

January 21st, 2021

5	
6	
7	
8	
9	
10	
11	
12pm	
1	
2	
3	
4	
5	
6	
7	
8	

PRIORITIES

TO DO

NOTES:

Friday

January 22nd, 2021

5	
6	
7	
8	
9	
10	
11	
12pm	
1	
2	
3	
4	
5	
6	
7	
8	

PRIORITIES

TO DO

NOTES:

Saturday

January 23rd, 2021

5	
6	
7	
8	
9	
10	
11	
12pm	
1	
2	
3	
4	
5	
6	
7	
8	

PRIORITIES

TO DO

NOTES:

Sunday

January 24th, 2021

5	
6	
7	
8	
9	
10	
11	
12pm	
1	
2	
3	
4	
5	
6	
7	
8	

PRIORITIES

TO DO

NOTES:

Monday

January 25th, 2021

5	
6	
7	
8	
9	
10	
11	
12pm	
1	
2	
3	
4	
5	
6	
7	
8	

PRIORITIES

TO DO

NOTES:

Tuesday

January 26th, 2021

5	
6	
7	
8	
9	
10	
11	
12pm	
1	
2	
3	
4	
5	
6	
7	
8	

PRIORITIES

TO DO

NOTES:

Wednesday

January 27th, 2021

5	
6	
7	
8	
9	
10	
11	
12pm	
1	
2	
3	
4	
5	
6	
7	
8	

PRIORITIES

TO DO

NOTES:

Thursday

January 28th, 2021

5	
6	
7	
8	
9	
10	
11	
12pm	
1	
2	
3	
4	
5	
6	
7	
8	

PRIORITIES

TO DO

NOTES:

Friday

January 29th, 2021

5	
6	
7	
8	
9	
10	
11	
12pm	
1	
2	
3	
4	
5	
6	
7	
8	

PRIORITIES

TO DO

NOTES:

Saturday

January 30th, 2021

5	
6	
7	
8	
9	
10	
11	
12pm	
1	
2	
3	
4	
5	
6	
7	
8	

PRIORITIES

TO DO

NOTES:

Sunday

January 31st, 2021

5	
6	
7	
8	
9	
10	
11	
12pm	
1	
2	
3	
4	
5	
6	
7	
8	

PRIORITIES

TO DO

NOTES:

Monday

February 1st, 2021

5	
6	
7	
8	
9	
10	
11	
12pm	
1	
2	
3	
4	
5	
6	
7	
8	

PRIORITIES

TO DO

NOTES:

Tuesday

February 2nd, 2021

5	
6	
7	
8	
9	
10	
11	
12pm	
1	
2	
3	
4	
5	
6	
7	
8	

PRIORITIES

TO DO

NOTES:

Wednesday

February 3rd, 2021

5	
6	
7	
8	
9	
10	
11	
12pm	
1	
2	
3	
4	
5	
6	
7	
8	

PRIORITIES

TO DO

NOTES:

Thursday

February 4th, 2021

5	
6	
7	
8	
9	
10	
11	
12pm	
1	
2	
3	
4	
5	
6	
7	
8	

PRIORITIES

TO DO

NOTES:

Friday

February 5th, 2021

5	
6	
7	
8	
9	
10	
11	
12pm	
1	
2	
3	
4	
5	
6	
7	
8	

PRIORITIES

TO DO

NOTES:

Saturday

February 6th, 2021

5	
6	
7	
8	
9	
10	
11	
12pm	
1	
2	
3	
4	
5	
6	
7	
8	

PRIORITIES

TO DO

NOTES:

Sunday

February 7th, 2021

5	
6	
7	
8	
9	
10	
11	
12pm	
1	
2	
3	
4	
5	
6	
7	
8	

PRIORITIES

TO DO

NOTES:

Monday

February 8th, 2021

5	
6	
7	
8	
9	
10	
11	
12pm	
1	
2	
3	
4	
5	
6	
7	
8	

PRIORITIES

TO DO

NOTES:

Tuesday

February 9th, 2021

5	
6	
7	
8	
9	
10	
11	
12pm	
1	
2	
3	
4	
5	
6	
7	
8	

PRIORITIES

TO DO

NOTES:

Wednesday

February 10th, 2021

5	
6	
7	
8	
9	
10	
11	
12pm	
1	
2	
3	
4	
5	
6	
7	
8	

PRIORITIES

TO DO

NOTES:

Thursday

February 11th, 2021

5	
6	
7	
8	
9	
10	
11	
12pm	
1	
2	
3	
4	
5	
6	
7	
8	

PRIORITIES

TO DO

NOTES:

Friday

February 12th, 2021

5	
6	
7	
8	
9	
10	
11	
12pm	
1	
2	
3	
4	
5	
6	
7	
8	

PRIORITIES

TO DO

NOTES:

Saturday

February 13th, 2021

5	
6	
7	
8	
9	
10	
11	
12pm	
1	
2	
3	
4	
5	
6	
7	
8	

PRIORITIES

TO DO

NOTES:

Sunday

February 14th, 2021

5	
6	
7	
8	
9	
10	
11	
12pm	
1	
2	
3	
4	
5	
6	
7	
8	

PRIORITIES

TO DO

NOTES:

Monday

February 15th, 2021

5	
6	
7	
8	
9	
10	
11	
12pm	
1	
2	
3	
4	
5	
6	
7	
8	

PRIORITIES

TO DO

NOTES:

Tuesday

February 16th, 2021

5	
6	
7	
8	
9	
10	
11	
12pm	
1	
2	
3	
4	
5	
6	
7	
8	

PRIORITIES

TO DO

NOTES:

Wednesday

February 17th, 2021

5	
6	
7	
8	
9	
10	
11	
12pm	
1	
2	
3	
4	
5	
6	
7	
8	

PRIORITIES

TO DO

NOTES:

Thursday

February 18th, 2021

5	
6	
7	
8	
9	
10	
11	
12pm	
1	
2	
3	
4	
5	
6	
7	
8	

PRIORITIES

TO DO

NOTES:

Friday

February 19th, 2021

5	
6	
7	
8	
9	
10	
11	
12pm	
1	
2	
3	
4	
5	
6	
7	
8	

PRIORITIES

TO DO

NOTES:

Saturday

February 20th, 2021

5	
6	
7	
8	
9	
10	
11	
12pm	
1	
2	
3	
4	
5	
6	
7	
8	

PRIORITIES

TO DO

NOTES:

Sunday

February 21st, 2021

5	
6	
7	
8	
9	
10	
11	
12pm	
1	
2	
3	
4	
5	
6	
7	
8	

PRIORITIES

TO DO

NOTES:

Monday

February 22nd, 2021

5	
6	
7	
8	
9	
10	
11	
12pm	
1	
2	
3	
4	
5	
6	
7	
8	

PRIORITIES

TO DO

NOTES:

Tuesday

February 23rd, 2021

5	
6	
7	
8	
9	
10	
11	
12pm	
1	
2	
3	
4	
5	
6	
7	
8	

PRIORITIES

TO DO

NOTES:

Wednesday

February 24th, 2021

5	
6	
7	
8	
9	
10	
11	
12pm	
1	
2	
3	
4	
5	
6	
7	
8	

PRIORITIES

TO DO

NOTES:

Thursday

February 25th, 2021

5	
6	
7	
8	
9	
10	
11	
12pm	
1	
2	
3	
4	
5	
6	
7	
8	

PRIORITIES

TO DO

NOTES:

Friday

February 26th, 2021

5	
6	
7	
8	
9	
10	
11	
12pm	
1	
2	
3	
4	
5	
6	
7	
8	

PRIORITIES

TO DO

NOTES:

Saturday

February 27th, 2021

5	
6	
7	
8	
9	
10	
11	
12pm	
1	
2	
3	
4	
5	
6	
7	
8	

PRIORITIES

TO DO

NOTES:

Sunday

February 28th, 2021

5	
6	
7	
8	
9	
10	
11	
12pm	
1	
2	
3	
4	
5	
6	
7	
8	

PRIORITIES

TO DO

NOTES:

Monday

March 1st, 2021

5	
6	
7	
8	
9	
10	
11	
12pm	
1	
2	
3	
4	
5	
6	
7	
8	

PRIORITIES

TO DO

NOTES:

Tuesday

March 2nd, 2021

5	
6	
7	
8	
9	
10	
11	
12pm	
1	
2	
3	
4	
5	
6	
7	
8	

PRIORITIES

TO DO

NOTES:

Wednesday

March 3rd, 2021

5	
6	
7	
8	
9	
10	
11	
12pm	
1	
2	
3	
4	
5	
6	
7	
8	

PRIORITIES

TO DO

NOTES:

Thursday

March 4th, 2021

5	
6	
7	
8	
9	
10	
11	
12pm	
1	
2	
3	
4	
5	
6	
7	
8	

PRIORITIES

TO DO

NOTES:

Friday

March 5th, 2021

5	
6	
7	
8	
9	
10	
11	
12pm	
1	
2	
3	
4	
5	
6	
7	
8	

PRIORITIES

TO DO

NOTES:

Saturday

March 6th, 2021

5	
6	
7	
8	
9	
10	
11	
12pm	
1	
2	
3	
4	
5	
6	
7	
8	

NOTES:

PRIORITIES

TO DO

Sunday

March 7th, 2021

5	
6	
7	
8	
9	
10	
11	
12pm	
1	
2	
3	
4	
5	
6	
7	
8	

PRIORITIES

TO DO

NOTES:

Monday

March 8th, 2021

5	
6	
7	
8	
9	
10	
11	
12pm	
1	
2	
3	
4	
5	
6	
7	
8	

PRIORITIES

TO DO

NOTES:

Tuesday

March 9th, 2021

5	
6	
7	
8	
9	
10	
11	
12pm	
1	
2	
3	
4	
5	
6	
7	
8	

PRIORITIES

TO DO

NOTES:

Wednesday

March 10th, 2021

5	
6	
7	
8	
9	
10	
11	
12pm	
1	
2	
3	
4	
5	
6	
7	
8	

PRIORITIES

TO DO

NOTES:

Thursday

March 11th, 2021

5	
6	
7	
8	
9	
10	
11	
12pm	
1	
2	
3	
4	
5	
6	
7	
8	

PRIORITIES

TO DO

NOTES:

Friday

March 12th, 2021

5	
6	
7	
8	
9	
10	
11	
12pm	
1	
2	
3	
4	
5	
6	
7	
8	

PRIORITIES

TO DO

NOTES:

Saturday

March 13th, 2021

5	
6	
7	
8	
9	
10	
11	
12pm	
1	
2	
3	
4	
5	
6	
7	
8	

PRIORITIES

TO DO

NOTES:

Sunday

March 14th, 2021

5	
6	
7	
8	
9	
10	
11	
12pm	
1	
2	
3	
4	
5	
6	
7	
8	

PRIORITIES

TO DO

NOTES:

Monday

March 15th, 2021

5	
6	
7	
8	
9	
10	
11	
12pm	
1	
2	
3	
4	
5	
6	
7	
8	

PRIORITIES

TO DO

NOTES:

Tuesday

March 16th, 2021

5	
6	
7	
8	
9	
10	
11	
12pm	
1	
2	
3	
4	
5	
6	
7	
8	

PRIORITIES

TO DO

NOTES:

Wednesday

March 17th, 2021

5	
6	
7	
8	
9	
10	
11	
12pm	
1	
2	
3	
4	
5	
6	
7	
8	

PRIORITIES

TO DO

NOTES:

Thursday

March 18th, 2021

5	
6	
7	
8	
9	
10	
11	
12pm	
1	
2	
3	
4	
5	
6	
7	
8	

PRIORITIES

TO DO

NOTES:

Friday

March 19th, 2021

5	
6	
7	
8	
9	
10	
11	
12pm	
1	
2	
3	
4	
5	
6	
7	
8	

PRIORITIES

TO DO

NOTES:

Saturday

March 20th, 2021

5	
6	
7	
8	
9	
10	
11	
12pm	
1	
2	
3	
4	
5	
6	
7	
8	

PRIORITIES

TO DO

NOTES:

Sunday

March 21st, 2021

5	
6	
7	
8	
9	
10	
11	
12pm	
1	
2	
3	
4	
5	
6	
7	
8	

PRIORITIES

TO DO

NOTES:

Monday

March 22nd, 2021

5	
6	
7	
8	
9	
10	
11	
12pm	
1	
2	
3	
4	
5	
6	
7	
8	

PRIORITIES

TO DO

NOTES:

Tuesday

March 23rd, 2021

5	
6	
7	
8	
9	
10	
11	
12pm	
1	
2	
3	
4	
5	
6	
7	
8	

PRIORITIES

TO DO

NOTES:

Wednesday

March 24th, 2021

5	
6	
7	
8	
9	
10	
11	
12pm	
1	
2	
3	
4	
5	
6	
7	
8	

PRIORITIES

TO DO

NOTES:

Thursday

March 25th, 2021

5	
6	
7	
8	
9	
10	
11	
12pm	
1	
2	
3	
4	
5	
6	
7	
8	

PRIORITIES

TO DO

NOTES:

Friday

March 26th, 2021

5	
6	
7	
8	
9	
10	
11	
12pm	
1	
2	
3	
4	
5	
6	
7	
8	

PRIORITIES

TO DO

NOTES:

Saturday

March 27th, 2021

5	
6	
7	
8	
9	
10	
11	
12pm	
1	
2	
3	
4	
5	
6	
7	
8	

PRIORITIES

TO DO

NOTES:

Sunday

March 28th, 2021

5	
6	
7	
8	
9	
10	
11	
12pm	
1	
2	
3	
4	
5	
6	
7	
8	

PRIORITIES

TO DO

NOTES:

Monday

March 29th, 2021

5	
6	
7	
8	
9	
10	
11	
12pm	
1	
2	
3	
4	
5	
6	
7	
8	

PRIORITIES

TO DO

NOTES:

Tuesday

March 30th, 2021

5	
6	
7	
8	
9	
10	
11	
12pm	
1	
2	
3	
4	
5	
6	
7	
8	

PRIORITIES

TO DO

NOTES:

Wednesday

March 31st, 2021

5	
6	
7	
8	
9	
10	
11	
12pm	
1	
2	
3	
4	
5	
6	
7	
8	

PRIORITIES

TO DO

NOTES:

Thursday

April 1st, 2021

5	
6	
7	
8	
9	
10	
11	
12pm	
1	
2	
3	
4	
5	
6	
7	
8	

PRIORITIES

TO DO

NOTES:

Friday

April 2nd, 2021

5	
6	
7	
8	
9	
10	
11	
12pm	
1	
2	
3	
4	
5	
6	
7	
8	

PRIORITIES

TO DO

NOTES:

Saturday

April 3rd, 2021

5	
6	
7	
8	
9	
10	
11	
12pm	
1	
2	
3	
4	
5	
6	
7	
8	

PRIORITIES

TO DO

NOTES:

Sunday

April 4th, 2021

5	
6	
7	
8	
9	
10	
11	
12pm	
1	
2	
3	
4	
5	
6	
7	
8	

PRIORITIES

TO DO

NOTES:

Monday

April 5th, 2021

5	
6	
7	
8	
9	
10	
11	
12pm	
1	
2	
3	
4	
5	
6	
7	
8	

PRIORITIES

TO DO

NOTES:

Tuesday

April 6th, 2021

5	
6	
7	
8	
9	
10	
11	
12pm	
1	
2	
3	
4	
5	
6	
7	
8	

PRIORITIES

TO DO

NOTES:

Wednesday

April 7th, 2021

5	
6	
7	
8	
9	
10	
11	
12pm	
1	
2	
3	
4	
5	
6	
7	
8	

PRIORITIES

TO DO

NOTES:

Thursday

April 8th, 2021

5	
6	
7	
8	
9	
10	
11	
12pm	
1	
2	
3	
4	
5	
6	
7	
8	

PRIORITIES

TO DO

NOTES:

Friday

April 9th, 2021

5	
6	
7	
8	
9	
10	
11	
12pm	
1	
2	
3	
4	
5	
6	
7	
8	

PRIORITIES

TO DO

NOTES:

Saturday

April 10th, 2021

5	
6	
7	
8	
9	
10	
11	
12pm	
1	
2	
3	
4	
5	
6	
7	
8	

PRIORITIES

TO DO

NOTES:

Sunday

April 11th, 2021

5	
6	
7	
8	
9	
10	
11	
12pm	
1	
2	
3	
4	
5	
6	
7	
8	

PRIORITIES

TO DO

NOTES:

Monday

April 12th, 2021

5	
6	
7	
8	
9	
10	
11	
12pm	
1	
2	
3	
4	
5	
6	
7	
8	

PRIORITIES

TO DO

NOTES:

Tuesday

April 13th, 2021

5	
6	
7	
8	
9	
10	
11	
12pm	
1	
2	
3	
4	
5	
6	
7	
8	

PRIORITIES

TO DO

NOTES:

Wednesday

April 14th, 2021

5	
6	
7	
8	
9	
10	
11	
12pm	
1	
2	
3	
4	
5	
6	
7	
8	

PRIORITIES

TO DO

NOTES:

Thursday

April 15th, 2021

5	
6	
7	
8	
9	
10	
11	
12pm	
1	
2	
3	
4	
5	
6	
7	
8	

PRIORITIES

TO DO

NOTES:

Friday

April 16th, 2021

5	
6	
7	
8	
9	
10	
11	
12pm	
1	
2	
3	
4	
5	
6	
7	
8	

PRIORITIES

TO DO

NOTES:

Saturday

April 17th, 2021

5	
6	
7	
8	
9	
10	
11	
12pm	
1	
2	
3	
4	
5	
6	
7	
8	

PRIORITIES

TO DO

NOTES:

Sunday

April 18th, 2021

5	
6	
7	
8	
9	
10	
11	
12pm	
1	
2	
3	
4	
5	
6	
7	
8	

PRIORITIES

TO DO

NOTES:

Monday

April 19th, 2021

5	
6	
7	
8	
9	
10	
11	
12pm	
1	
2	
3	
4	
5	
6	
7	
8	

PRIORITIES

TO DO

NOTES:

Tuesday

April 20th, 2021

5	
6	
7	
8	
9	
10	
11	
12pm	
1	
2	
3	
4	
5	
6	
7	
8	

PRIORITIES

TO DO

NOTES:

Wednesday

April 21st, 2021

5	
6	
7	
8	
9	
10	
11	
12pm	
1	
2	
3	
4	
5	
6	
7	
8	

PRIORITIES

TO DO

NOTES:

Thursday

April 22nd, 2021

5	
6	
7	
8	
9	
10	
11	
12pm	
1	
2	
3	
4	
5	
6	
7	
8	

PRIORITIES

TO DO

NOTES:

Friday

April 23rd, 2021

5	
6	
7	
8	
9	
10	
11	
12pm	
1	
2	
3	
4	
5	
6	
7	
8	

PRIORITIES

TO DO

NOTES:

Saturday

April 24th, 2021

5	
6	
7	
8	
9	
10	
11	
12pm	
1	
2	
3	
4	
5	
6	
7	
8	

PRIORITIES

TO DO

NOTES:

Sunday

April 25th, 2021

5	
6	
7	
8	
9	
10	
11	
12pm	
1	
2	
3	
4	
5	
6	
7	
8	

PRIORITIES

TO DO

NOTES:

Monday

April 26th, 2021

5	
6	
7	
8	
9	
10	
11	
12pm	
1	
2	
3	
4	
5	
6	
7	
8	

PRIORITIES

TO DO

NOTES:

Tuesday

April 27th, 2021

5	
6	
7	
8	
9	
10	
11	
12pm	
1	
2	
3	
4	
5	
6	
7	
8	

PRIORITIES

TO DO

NOTES:

Wednesday

April 28th, 2021

5	
6	
7	
8	
9	
10	
11	
12pm	
1	
2	
3	
4	
5	
6	
7	
8	

PRIORITIES

TO DO

NOTES:

Thursday

April 29th, 2021

5	
6	
7	
8	
9	
10	
11	
12pm	
1	
2	
3	
4	
5	
6	
7	
8	

PRIORITIES

TO DO

NOTES:

Friday

April 30th, 2021

5	
6	
7	
8	
9	
10	
11	
12pm	
1	
2	
3	
4	
5	
6	
7	
8	

PRIORITIES

TO DO

NOTES:

Saturday

May 1st, 2021

5	
6	
7	
8	
9	
10	
11	
12pm	
1	
2	
3	
4	
5	
6	
7	
8	

PRIORITIES

TO DO

NOTES:

Sunday

May 2nd, 2021

5	
6	
7	
8	
9	
10	
11	
12pm	
1	
2	
3	
4	
5	
6	
7	
8	

PRIORITIES

TO DO

NOTES:

Monday

May 3rd, 2021

5	
6	
7	
8	
9	
10	
11	
12pm	
1	
2	
3	
4	
5	
6	
7	
8	

PRIORITIES

TO DO

NOTES:

Tuesday

May 4th, 2021

5	
6	
7	
8	
9	
10	
11	
12pm	
1	
2	
3	
4	
5	
6	
7	
8	

PRIORITIES

TO DO

NOTES:

Wednesday

May 5th, 2021

5	
6	
7	
8	
9	
10	
11	
12pm	
1	
2	
3	
4	
5	
6	
7	
8	

PRIORITIES

TO DO

NOTES:

Thursday

May 6th, 2021

5	
6	
7	
8	
9	
10	
11	
12pm	
1	
2	
3	
4	
5	
6	
7	
8	

PRIORITIES

TO DO

NOTES:

Friday

May 7th, 2021

5	
6	
7	
8	
9	
10	
11	
12pm	
1	
2	
3	
4	
5	
6	
7	
8	

PRIORITIES

TO DO

NOTES:

Saturday

May 8th, 2021

5	
6	
7	
8	
9	
10	
11	
12pm	
1	
2	
3	
4	
5	
6	
7	
8	

PRIORITIES

TO DO

NOTES:

Sunday

May 9th, 2021

5	
6	
7	
8	
9	
10	
11	
12pm	
1	
2	
3	
4	
5	
6	
7	
8	

PRIORITIES

TO DO

NOTES:

Monday

May 10th, 2021

5	
6	
7	
8	
9	
10	
11	
12pm	
1	
2	
3	
4	
5	
6	
7	
8	

PRIORITIES

TO DO

NOTES:

Tuesday

May 11th, 2021

5	
6	
7	
8	
9	
10	
11	
12pm	
1	
2	
3	
4	
5	
6	
7	
8	

PRIORITIES

TO DO

NOTES:

Wednesday

May 12th, 2021

5	
6	
7	
8	
9	
10	
11	
12pm	
1	
2	
3	
4	
5	
6	
7	
8	

PRIORITIES

TO DO

NOTES:

Thursday

May 13th, 2021

5	
6	
7	
8	
9	
10	
11	
12pm	
1	
2	
3	
4	
5	
6	
7	
8	

PRIORITIES

TO DO

NOTES:

Friday

May 14th, 2021

5	
6	
7	
8	
9	
10	
11	
12pm	
1	
2	
3	
4	
5	
6	
7	
8	

PRIORITIES

TO DO

NOTES:

Saturday

May 15th, 2021

5	
6	
7	
8	
9	
10	
11	
12pm	
1	
2	
3	
4	
5	
6	
7	
8	

PRIORITIES

TO DO

NOTES:

Sunday

May 16th, 2021

5	
6	
7	
8	
9	
10	
11	
12pm	
1	
2	
3	
4	
5	
6	
7	
8	

PRIORITIES

TO DO

NOTES:

Monday

May 17th, 2021

5	
6	
7	
8	
9	
10	
11	
12pm	
1	
2	
3	
4	
5	
6	
7	
8	

PRIORITIES

TO DO

NOTES:

Tuesday

May 18th, 2021

5	
6	
7	
8	
9	
10	
11	
12pm	
1	
2	
3	
4	
5	
6	
7	
8	

PRIORITIES

TO DO

NOTES:

Wednesday

May 19th, 2021

5	
6	
7	
8	
9	
10	
11	
12pm	
1	
2	
3	
4	
5	
6	
7	
8	

PRIORITIES

TO DO

NOTES:

Thursday

May 20th, 2021

5	
6	
7	
8	
9	
10	
11	
12pm	
1	
2	
3	
4	
5	
6	
7	
8	

PRIORITIES

TO DO

NOTES:

Friday

May 21st, 2021

5	
6	
7	
8	
9	
10	
11	
12pm	
1	
2	
3	
4	
5	
6	
7	
8	

PRIORITIES

TO DO

NOTES:

Saturday

May 22nd, 2021

5	
6	
7	
8	
9	
10	
11	
12pm	
1	
2	
3	
4	
5	
6	
7	
8	

PRIORITIES

TO DO

NOTES:

Sunday

May 23rd, 2021

5	
6	
7	
8	
9	
10	
11	
12pm	
1	
2	
3	
4	
5	
6	
7	
8	

PRIORITIES

TO DO

NOTES:

Monday

May 24th, 2021

5	
6	
7	
8	
9	
10	
11	
12pm	
1	
2	
3	
4	
5	
6	
7	
8	

PRIORITIES

TO DO

NOTES:

Tuesday

May 25th, 2021

5	
6	
7	
8	
9	
10	
11	
12pm	
1	
2	
3	
4	
5	
6	
7	
8	

PRIORITIES

TO DO

NOTES:

Wednesday

May 26th, 2021

5	
6	
7	
8	
9	
10	
11	
12pm	
1	
2	
3	
4	
5	
6	
7	
8	

PRIORITIES

TO DO

NOTES:

Thursday

May 27th, 2021

5	
6	
7	
8	
9	
10	
11	
12pm	
1	
2	
3	
4	
5	
6	
7	
8	

PRIORITIES

TO DO

NOTES:

Friday

May 28th, 2021

5	
6	
7	
8	
9	
10	
11	
12pm	
1	
2	
3	
4	
5	
6	
7	
8	

PRIORITIES

TO DO

NOTES:

Saturday

May 29th, 2021

5	
6	
7	
8	
9	
10	
11	
12pm	
1	
2	
3	
4	
5	
6	
7	
8	

PRIORITIES

TO DO

NOTES:

Sunday

May 30th, 2021

5	
6	
7	
8	
9	
10	
11	
12pm	
1	
2	
3	
4	
5	
6	
7	
8	

PRIORITIES

TO DO

NOTES:

Monday

May 31st, 2021

5	
6	
7	
8	
9	
10	
11	
12pm	
1	
2	
3	
4	
5	
6	
7	
8	

PRIORITIES

TO DO

NOTES:

Tuesday

June 1st, 2021

5	
6	
7	
8	
9	
10	
11	
12pm	
1	
2	
3	
4	
5	
6	
7	
8	

PRIORITIES

TO DO

NOTES:

Wednesday

June 2nd, 2021

5	
6	
7	
8	
9	
10	
11	
12pm	
1	
2	
3	
4	
5	
6	
7	
8	

PRIORITIES

TO DO

NOTES:

Thursday

June 3rd, 2021

5	
6	
7	
8	
9	
10	
11	
12pm	
1	
2	
3	
4	
5	
6	
7	
8	

PRIORITIES

TO DO

NOTES:

Friday

June 4th, 2021

5	
6	
7	
8	
9	
10	
11	
12pm	
1	
2	
3	
4	
5	
6	
7	
8	

PRIORITIES

TO DO

NOTES:

Saturday

June 5th, 2021

5	
6	
7	
8	
9	
10	
11	
12pm	
1	
2	
3	
4	
5	
6	
7	
8	

PRIORITIES

TO DO

NOTES:

Sunday

June 6th, 2021

5	
6	
7	
8	
9	
10	
11	
12pm	
1	
2	
3	
4	
5	
6	
7	
8	

PRIORITIES

TO DO

NOTES:

Monday

June 7th, 2021

5	
6	
7	
8	
9	
10	
11	
12pm	
1	
2	
3	
4	
5	
6	
7	
8	

PRIORITIES

TO DO

NOTES:

Tuesday

June 8th, 2021

5	
6	
7	
8	
9	
10	
11	
12pm	
1	
2	
3	
4	
5	
6	
7	
8	

PRIORITIES

TO DO

NOTES:

Wednesday

June 9th, 2021

5	
6	
7	
8	
9	
10	
11	
12pm	
1	
2	
3	
4	
5	
6	
7	
8	

PRIORITIES

TO DO

NOTES:

Thursday

June 10th, 2021

5	
6	
7	
8	
9	
10	
11	
12pm	
1	
2	
3	
4	
5	
6	
7	
8	

PRIORITIES

TO DO

NOTES:

Friday

June 11th, 2021

5	
6	
7	
8	
9	
10	
11	
12pm	
1	
2	
3	
4	
5	
6	
7	
8	

PRIORITIES

TO DO

NOTES:

Saturday

June 12th, 2021

5	
6	
7	
8	
9	
10	
11	
12pm	
1	
2	
3	
4	
5	
6	
7	
8	

PRIORITIES

TO DO

NOTES:

Sunday

June 13th, 2021

5	
6	
7	
8	
9	
10	
11	
12pm	
1	
2	
3	
4	
5	
6	
7	
8	

PRIORITIES

TO DO

NOTES:

Monday

June 14th, 2021

5	
6	
7	
8	
9	
10	
11	
12pm	
1	
2	
3	
4	
5	
6	
7	
8	

PRIORITIES

TO DO

NOTES:

Tuesday

June 15th, 2021

5	
6	
7	
8	
9	
10	
11	
12pm	
1	
2	
3	
4	
5	
6	
7	
8	

PRIORITIES

TO DO

NOTES:

Wednesday

June 16th, 2021

5	
6	
7	
8	
9	
10	
11	
12pm	
1	
2	
3	
4	
5	
6	
7	
8	

PRIORITIES

TO DO

NOTES:

Thursday

June 17th, 2021

5	
6	
7	
8	
9	
10	
11	
12pm	
1	
2	
3	
4	
5	
6	
7	
8	

PRIORITIES

TO DO

NOTES:

Friday

June 18th, 2021

5	
6	
7	
8	
9	
10	
11	
12pm	
1	
2	
3	
4	
5	
6	
7	
8	

PRIORITIES

TO DO

NOTES:

Saturday

June 19th, 2021

5	
6	
7	
8	
9	
10	
11	
12pm	
1	
2	
3	
4	
5	
6	
7	
8	

PRIORITIES

TO DO

NOTES:

Sunday

June 20th, 2021

5	
6	
7	
8	
9	
10	
11	
12pm	
1	
2	
3	
4	
5	
6	
7	
8	

PRIORITIES

TO DO

NOTES:

Monday

June 21st, 2021

5	
6	
7	
8	
9	
10	
11	
12pm	
1	
2	
3	
4	
5	
6	
7	
8	

PRIORITIES

TO DO

NOTES:

Tuesday

June 22nd, 2021

5	
6	
7	
8	
9	
10	
11	
12pm	
1	
2	
3	
4	
5	
6	
7	
8	

PRIORITIES

TO DO

NOTES:

Wednesday

June 23rd, 2021

5	
6	
7	
8	
9	
10	
11	
12pm	
1	
2	
3	
4	
5	
6	
7	
8	

PRIORITIES

TO DO

NOTES:

Thursday

June 24th, 2021

5	
6	
7	
8	
9	
10	
11	
12pm	
1	
2	
3	
4	
5	
6	
7	
8	

PRIORITIES

TO DO

NOTES:

Friday

June 25th, 2021

5	
6	
7	
8	
9	
10	
11	
12pm	
1	
2	
3	
4	
5	
6	
7	
8	

PRIORITIES

TO DO

NOTES:

Saturday

June 26th, 2021

5	
6	
7	
8	
9	
10	
11	
12pm	
1	
2	
3	
4	
5	
6	
7	
8	

PRIORITIES

TO DO

NOTES:

Sunday

June 27th, 2021

5	
6	
7	
8	
9	
10	
11	
12pm	
1	
2	
3	
4	
5	
6	
7	
8	

PRIORITIES

TO DO

NOTES:

Monday

June 28th, 2021

5	
6	
7	
8	
9	
10	
11	
12pm	
1	
2	
3	
4	
5	
6	
7	
8	

PRIORITIES

TO DO

NOTES:

Tuesday

June 29th, 2021

5	
6	
7	
8	
9	
10	
11	
12pm	
1	
2	
3	
4	
5	
6	
7	
8	

PRIORITIES

TO DO

NOTES:

Wednesday

June 30th, 2021

5	
6	
7	
8	
9	
10	
11	
12pm	
1	
2	
3	
4	
5	
6	
7	
8	

PRIORITIES

TO DO

NOTES:

Thursday

July 1st, 2021

5	
6	
7	
8	
9	
10	
11	
12pm	
1	
2	
3	
4	
5	
6	
7	
8	

PRIORITIES

TO DO

NOTES:

Friday

July 2nd, 2021

5	
6	
7	
8	
9	
10	
11	
12pm	
1	
2	
3	
4	
5	
6	
7	
8	

PRIORITIES

TO DO

NOTES:

Saturday

July 3rd, 2021

5	
6	
7	
8	
9	
10	
11	
12pm	
1	
2	
3	
4	
5	
6	
7	
8	

PRIORITIES

TO DO

NOTES:

Sunday

July 4th, 2021

5	
6	
7	
8	
9	
10	
11	
12pm	
1	
2	
3	
4	
5	
6	
7	
8	

PRIORITIES

TO DO

NOTES:

Monday

July 5th, 2021

5	
6	
7	
8	
9	
10	
11	
12pm	
1	
2	
3	
4	
5	
6	
7	
8	

PRIORITIES

TO DO

NOTES:

Tuesday

July 6th, 2021

5	
6	
7	
8	
9	
10	
11	
12pm	
1	
2	
3	
4	
5	
6	
7	
8	

PRIORITIES

TO DO

NOTES:

Wednesday

July 7th, 2021

5	
6	
7	
8	
9	
10	
11	
12pm	
1	
2	
3	
4	
5	
6	
7	
8	

PRIORITIES

TO DO

NOTES:

Thursday

July 8th, 2021

5	
6	
7	
8	
9	
10	
11	
12pm	
1	
2	
3	
4	
5	
6	
7	
8	

PRIORITIES

TO DO

NOTES:

Friday

July 9th, 2021

5	
6	
7	
8	
9	
10	
11	
12pm	
1	
2	
3	
4	
5	
6	
7	
8	

PRIORITIES

TO DO

NOTES:

Saturday

July 10th, 2021

5	
6	
7	
8	
9	
10	
11	
12pm	
1	
2	
3	
4	
5	
6	
7	
8	

PRIORITIES

TO DO

NOTES:

Sunday

July 11th, 2021

5	
6	
7	
8	
9	
10	
11	
12pm	
1	
2	
3	
4	
5	
6	
7	
8	

PRIORITIES

TO DO

NOTES:

Monday

July 12th, 2021

5	
6	
7	
8	
9	
10	
11	
12pm	
1	
2	
3	
4	
5	
6	
7	
8	

PRIORITIES

TO DO

NOTES:

Tuesday

July 13th, 2021

5	
6	
7	
8	
9	
10	
11	
12pm	
1	
2	
3	
4	
5	
6	
7	
8	

PRIORITIES

TO DO

NOTES:

Wednesday

July 14th, 2021

5	
6	
7	
8	
9	
10	
11	
12pm	
1	
2	
3	
4	
5	
6	
7	
8	

PRIORITIES

TO DO

NOTES:

Thursday

July 15th, 2021

5	
6	
7	
8	
9	
10	
11	
12pm	
1	
2	
3	
4	
5	
6	
7	
8	

PRIORITIES

TO DO

NOTES:

Friday

July 16th, 2021

5	
6	
7	
8	
9	
10	
11	
12pm	
1	
2	
3	
4	
5	
6	
7	
8	

PRIORITIES

TO DO

NOTES:

Saturday

July 17th, 2021

5	
6	
7	
8	
9	
10	
11	
12pm	
1	
2	
3	
4	
5	
6	
7	
8	

PRIORITIES

TO DO

NOTES:

Sunday

July 18th, 2021

5	
6	
7	
8	
9	
10	
11	
12pm	
1	
2	
3	
4	
5	
6	
7	
8	

PRIORITIES

TO DO

NOTES:

Monday

July 19th, 2021

5	
6	
7	
8	
9	
10	
11	
12pm	
1	
2	
3	
4	
5	
6	
7	
8	

PRIORITIES

TO DO

NOTES:

Tuesday

July 20th, 2021

5	
6	
7	
8	
9	
10	
11	
12pm	
1	
2	
3	
4	
5	
6	
7	
8	

PRIORITIES

TO DO

NOTES:

Wednesday

July 21st, 2021

5	
6	
7	
8	
9	
10	
11	
12pm	
1	
2	
3	
4	
5	
6	
7	
8	

PRIORITIES

TO DO

NOTES:

Thursday

July 22nd, 2021

5	
6	
7	
8	
9	
10	
11	
12pm	
1	
2	
3	
4	
5	
6	
7	
8	

PRIORITIES

TO DO

NOTES:

Friday

July 23rd, 2021

5	
6	
7	
8	
9	
10	
11	
12pm	
1	
2	
3	
4	
5	
6	
7	
8	

PRIORITIES

TO DO

NOTES:

Saturday

July 24th, 2021

5	
6	
7	
8	
9	
10	
11	
12pm	
1	
2	
3	
4	
5	
6	
7	
8	

PRIORITIES

TO DO

NOTES:

Sunday

July 25th, 2021

5	
6	
7	
8	
9	
10	
11	
12pm	
1	
2	
3	
4	
5	
6	
7	
8	

PRIORITIES

TO DO

NOTES:

Monday

July 26th, 2021

5	
6	
7	
8	
9	
10	
11	
12pm	
1	
2	
3	
4	
5	
6	
7	
8	

PRIORITIES

TO DO

NOTES:

Tuesday

July 27th, 2021

5	
6	
7	
8	
9	
10	
11	
12pm	
1	
2	
3	
4	
5	
6	
7	
8	

PRIORITIES

TO DO

NOTES:

Wednesday

July 28th, 2021

5	
6	
7	
8	
9	
10	
11	
12pm	
1	
2	
3	
4	
5	
6	
7	
8	

PRIORITIES

TO DO

NOTES:

Thursday

July 29th, 2021

5	
6	
7	
8	
9	
10	
11	
12pm	
1	
2	
3	
4	
5	
6	
7	
8	

PRIORITIES

TO DO

NOTES:

Friday

July 30th, 2021

5	
6	
7	
8	
9	
10	
11	
12pm	
1	
2	
3	
4	
5	
6	
7	
8	

PRIORITIES

TO DO

NOTES:

Saturday

July 31st, 2021

5	
6	
7	
8	
9	
10	
11	
12pm	
1	
2	
3	
4	
5	
6	
7	
8	

PRIORITIES

TO DO

NOTES:

Sunday

August 1st, 2021

5	
6	
7	
8	
9	
10	
11	
12pm	
1	
2	
3	
4	
5	
6	
7	
8	

PRIORITIES

TO DO

NOTES:

Monday

August 2nd, 2021

5	
6	
7	
8	
9	
10	
11	
12pm	
1	
2	
3	
4	
5	
6	
7	
8	

PRIORITIES

TO DO

NOTES:

Tuesday

August 3rd, 2021

5	
6	
7	
8	
9	
10	
11	
12pm	
1	
2	
3	
4	
5	
6	
7	
8	

PRIORITIES

TO DO

NOTES:

Wednesday

August 4th, 2021

5	
6	
7	
8	
9	
10	
11	
12pm	
1	
2	
3	
4	
5	
6	
7	
8	

PRIORITIES

TO DO

NOTES:

Thursday

August 5th, 2021

5	
6	
7	
8	
9	
10	
11	
12pm	
1	
2	
3	
4	
5	
6	
7	
8	

PRIORITIES

TO DO

NOTES:

Friday

August 6th, 2021

5	
6	
7	
8	
9	
10	
11	
12pm	
1	
2	
3	
4	
5	
6	
7	
8	

PRIORITIES

TO DO

NOTES:

Saturday

August 7th, 2021

5	
6	
7	
8	
9	
10	
11	
12pm	
1	
2	
3	
4	
5	
6	
7	
8	

PRIORITIES

TO DO

NOTES:

Sunday

August 8th, 2021

5	
6	
7	
8	
9	
10	
11	
12pm	
1	
2	
3	
4	
5	
6	
7	
8	

PRIORITIES

TO DO

NOTES:

Monday

August 9th, 2021

5	
6	
7	
8	
9	
10	
11	
12pm	
1	
2	
3	
4	
5	
6	
7	
8	

PRIORITIES

TO DO

NOTES:

Tuesday

August 10th, 2021

5	
6	
7	
8	
9	
10	
11	
12pm	
1	
2	
3	
4	
5	
6	
7	
8	

PRIORITIES

TO DO

NOTES:

Wednesday

August 11th, 2021

5	
6	
7	
8	
9	
10	
11	
12pm	
1	
2	
3	
4	
5	
6	
7	
8	

PRIORITIES

TO DO

NOTES:

Thursday

August 12th, 2021

5	
6	
7	
8	
9	
10	
11	
12pm	
1	
2	
3	
4	
5	
6	
7	
8	

PRIORITIES

TO DO

NOTES:

Friday

August 13th, 2021

5	
6	
7	
8	
9	
10	
11	
12pm	
1	
2	
3	
4	
5	
6	
7	
8	

PRIORITIES

TO DO

NOTES:

Saturday

August 14th, 2021

5	
6	
7	
8	
9	
10	
11	
12pm	
1	
2	
3	
4	
5	
6	
7	
8	

PRIORITIES

TO DO

NOTES:

Sunday

August 15th, 2021

5	
6	
7	
8	
9	
10	
11	
12pm	
1	
2	
3	
4	
5	
6	
7	
8	

PRIORITIES

TO DO

NOTES:

Monday

August 16th, 2021

5	
6	
7	
8	
9	
10	
11	
12pm	
1	
2	
3	
4	
5	
6	
7	
8	

PRIORITIES

TO DO

NOTES:

Tuesday

August 17th, 2021

5	
6	
7	
8	
9	
10	
11	
12pm	
1	
2	
3	
4	
5	
6	
7	
8	

PRIORITIES

TO DO

NOTES:

Wednesday

August 18th, 2021

5	
6	
7	
8	
9	
10	
11	
12pm	
1	
2	
3	
4	
5	
6	
7	
8	

PRIORITIES

TO DO

NOTES:

Thursday

August 19th, 2021

5	
6	
7	
8	
9	
10	
11	
12pm	
1	
2	
3	
4	
5	
6	
7	
8	

PRIORITIES

TO DO

NOTES:

Friday

August 20th, 2021

5	
6	
7	
8	
9	
10	
11	
12pm	
1	
2	
3	
4	
5	
6	
7	
8	

PRIORITIES

TO DO

NOTES:

Saturday

August 21st, 2021

5	
6	
7	
8	
9	
10	
11	
12pm	
1	
2	
3	
4	
5	
6	
7	
8	

PRIORITIES

TO DO

NOTES:

Sunday

August 22nd, 2021

5	
6	
7	
8	
9	
10	
11	
12pm	
1	
2	
3	
4	
5	
6	
7	
8	

PRIORITIES

TO DO

NOTES:

Monday

August 23rd, 2021

5	
6	
7	
8	
9	
10	
11	
12pm	
1	
2	
3	
4	
5	
6	
7	
8	

PRIORITIES

TO DO

NOTES:

Tuesday

August 24th, 2021

5	
6	
7	
8	
9	
10	
11	
12pm	
1	
2	
3	
4	
5	
6	
7	
8	

PRIORITIES

TO DO

NOTES:

Wednesday

August 25th, 2021

5	
6	
7	
8	
9	
10	
11	
12pm	
1	
2	
3	
4	
5	
6	
7	
8	

PRIORITIES

TO DO

NOTES:

Thursday

August 26th, 2021

5	
6	
7	
8	
9	
10	
11	
12pm	
1	
2	
3	
4	
5	
6	
7	
8	

PRIORITIES

TO DO

NOTES:

Friday

August 27th, 2021

5	
6	
7	
8	
9	
10	
11	
12pm	
1	
2	
3	
4	
5	
6	
7	
8	

PRIORITIES

TO DO

NOTES:

Saturday

August 28th, 2021

5	
6	
7	
8	
9	
10	
11	
12pm	
1	
2	
3	
4	
5	
6	
7	
8	

PRIORITIES

TO DO

NOTES:

Sunday

August 29th, 2021

5	
6	
7	
8	
9	
10	
11	
12pm	
1	
2	
3	
4	
5	
6	
7	
8	

PRIORITIES

TO DO

NOTES:

Monday

August 30th, 2021

5	
6	
7	
8	
9	
10	
11	
12pm	
1	
2	
3	
4	
5	
6	
7	
8	

PRIORITIES

TO DO

NOTES:

Tuesday

August 31st, 2021

5	
6	
7	
8	
9	
10	
11	
12pm	
1	
2	
3	
4	
5	
6	
7	
8	

PRIORITIES

TO DO

NOTES:

Wednesday

September 1st, 2021

5	
6	
7	
8	
9	
10	
11	
12pm	
1	
2	
3	
4	
5	
6	
7	
8	

PRIORITIES

TO DO

NOTES:

Thursday

September 2nd, 2021

5	
6	
7	
8	
9	
10	
11	
12pm	
1	
2	
3	
4	
5	
6	
7	
8	

PRIORITIES

TO DO

NOTES:

Friday

September 3rd, 2021

5	
6	
7	
8	
9	
10	
11	
12pm	
1	
2	
3	
4	
5	
6	
7	
8	

PRIORITIES

TO DO

NOTES:

Saturday

September 4th, 2021

5	
6	
7	
8	
9	
10	
11	
12pm	
1	
2	
3	
4	
5	
6	
7	
8	

PRIORITIES

TO DO

NOTES:

Sunday

September 5th, 2021

5	
6	
7	
8	
9	
10	
11	
12pm	
1	
2	
3	
4	
5	
6	
7	
8	

PRIORITIES

TO DO

NOTES:

Monday

September 6th, 2021

5	
6	
7	
8	
9	
10	
11	
12pm	
1	
2	
3	
4	
5	
6	
7	
8	

PRIORITIES

TO DO

NOTES:

Tuesday

September 7th, 2021

5	
6	
7	
8	
9	
10	
11	
12pm	
1	
2	
3	
4	
5	
6	
7	
8	

PRIORITIES

TO DO

NOTES:

Wednesday

September 8th, 2021

5	
6	
7	
8	
9	
10	
11	
12pm	
1	
2	
3	
4	
5	
6	
7	
8	

PRIORITIES

TO DO

NOTES:

Thursday

September 9th, 2021

5	
6	
7	
8	
9	
10	
11	
12pm	
1	
2	
3	
4	
5	
6	
7	
8	

PRIORITIES

TO DO

NOTES:

Friday

September 10th, 2021

5	
6	
7	
8	
9	
10	
11	
12pm	
1	
2	
3	
4	
5	
6	
7	
8	

PRIORITIES

TO DO

NOTES:

Saturday

September 11th, 2021

5	
6	
7	
8	
9	
10	
11	
12pm	
1	
2	
3	
4	
5	
6	
7	
8	

PRIORITIES

TO DO

NOTES:

Sunday

September 12th, 2021

5	
6	
7	
8	
9	
10	
11	
12pm	
1	
2	
3	
4	
5	
6	
7	
8	

PRIORITIES

TO DO

NOTES:

Monday

September 13th, 2021

5	
6	
7	
8	
9	
10	
11	
12pm	
1	
2	
3	
4	
5	
6	
7	
8	

NOTES:

PRIORITIES

TO DO

Tuesday

September 14th, 2021

5	
6	
7	
8	
9	
10	
11	
12pm	
1	
2	
3	
4	
5	
6	
7	
8	

PRIORITIES

TO DO

NOTES:

Wednesday

September 15th, 2021

5	
6	
7	
8	
9	
10	
11	
12pm	
1	
2	
3	
4	
5	
6	
7	
8	

PRIORITIES

TO DO

NOTES:

Thursday

September 16th, 2021

5	
6	
7	
8	
9	
10	
11	
12pm	
1	
2	
3	
4	
5	
6	
7	
8	

PRIORITIES

TO DO

NOTES:

Friday

September 17th, 2021

5	
6	
7	
8	
9	
10	
11	
12pm	
1	
2	
3	
4	
5	
6	
7	
8	

PRIORITIES

TO DO

NOTES:

Saturday

September 18th, 2021

5	
6	
7	
8	
9	
10	
11	
12pm	
1	
2	
3	
4	
5	
6	
7	
8	

PRIORITIES

TO DO

NOTES:

Sunday

September 19th, 2021

5	
6	
7	
8	
9	
10	
11	
12pm	
1	
2	
3	
4	
5	
6	
7	
8	

PRIORITIES

TO DO

NOTES:

Monday

September 20th, 2021

5	
6	
7	
8	
9	
10	
11	
12pm	
1	
2	
3	
4	
5	
6	
7	
8	

PRIORITIES

TO DO

NOTES:

Tuesday

September 21st, 2021

5	
6	
7	
8	
9	
10	
11	
12pm	
1	
2	
3	
4	
5	
6	
7	
8	

PRIORITIES

TO DO

NOTES:

Wednesday

September 22nd, 2021

5	
6	
7	
8	
9	
10	
11	
12pm	
1	
2	
3	
4	
5	
6	
7	
8	

PRIORITIES

TO DO

NOTES:

Thursday

September 23rd, 2021

5	
6	
7	
8	
9	
10	
11	
12pm	
1	
2	
3	
4	
5	
6	
7	
8	

PRIORITIES

TO DO

NOTES:

Friday

September 24th, 2021

5	
6	
7	
8	
9	
10	
11	
12pm	
1	
2	
3	
4	
5	
6	
7	
8	

PRIORITIES

TO DO

NOTES:

Saturday

September 25th, 2021

5	
6	
7	
8	
9	
10	
11	
12pm	
1	
2	
3	
4	
5	
6	
7	
8	

PRIORITIES

TO DO

NOTES:

Sunday

September 26th, 2021

5	
6	
7	
8	
9	
10	
11	
12pm	
1	
2	
3	
4	
5	
6	
7	
8	

PRIORITIES

TO DO

NOTES:

Monday

September 27th, 2021

5	
6	
7	
8	
9	
10	
11	
12pm	
1	
2	
3	
4	
5	
6	
7	
8	

PRIORITIES

TO DO

NOTES:

Tuesday

September 28th, 2021

5	
6	
7	
8	
9	
10	
11	
12pm	
1	
2	
3	
4	
5	
6	
7	
8	

PRIORITIES

TO DO

NOTES:

Wednesday

September 29th, 2021

5	
6	
7	
8	
9	
10	
11	
12pm	
1	
2	
3	
4	
5	
6	
7	
8	

PRIORITIES

TO DO

NOTES:

CPSIA information can be obtained
at www.ICGtesting.com
Printed in the USA
LVHW100703190121
676856LV00010B/413